As Louis XIV's finance minister Colbert predicted, the Sun King's reign was measured, not by magnificent acts of warfare, but by the supreme symbol of that monarch's splendour, Versailles and its gardens.

This collection of images provides the most sensual and spiritually compelling illustration of those gardens imaginable. You will find in it — to quote a seventeenth-century guidebook — 'a wild solitude that would not displease you', and at the same time you will agree with the Duc de Saint-Simon's verdict of 1700: 'Not Asia, nor antiquity, could show anything more vast, grandiose and elaborate than these gardens.'

JOHN LORING

# The Gardens of Versailles

Jean-Baptiste Leroux

# The Gardens _of_ Versailles

Translated from the French by Alexis Gregory

First published in the United Kingdom in 2002 by
Thames & Hudson Ltd, 181A High Holborn, London WC1V 7QX

www.thamesandhudson.com

British Library Cataloguing-in-Publication Data
A catalogue record for this book is available from the British Library

ISBN 0-500-28390-7

Printed in Italy

# Contents

# Preface

THE GARDENS OF VERSAILLES know no equal as a monument to the tenuous alliance of Man and Nature. Here, over three hundred years ago, 'The Sun King' Louis XIV commanded an army of architects, masons, sculptors, hydraulic engineers and gardeners to impose order on Nature's unbridled chaos, to create a Heaven on Earth, a second paradise far grander than Eden and, unlike Eden, based on human logic, art and science. Here, for over three hundred years, Nature, wearing not Louis's but her own mask of the Sun, has played games with the imperious king's Versailles, illuminating his operatic works in a blaze of glorious light or alternately obscuring them in shadow.

In her army of accomplices, Nature commands the four seasons as well as platoons of water spirits and phalanxes of more specialized deities who transform the Sun King's so grand and marvellous gardens as the spirit moves them, wrapping them in clouds, enveloping them in frost, recklessly tossing about their stately allées* of trees with storms or softening the formality of their parterres with gentle rains.

Louis XIV's courtiers were witnesses to this pageant of their king's and Nature's alternating alliances and battles, of the shifts from harmony to struggle, of their masks and disguises, each determined to dominate and, at times, to run roughshod over the other; Nature the obvious and ultimate victor imposing her own, not Louis's, harmony.

The court is long gone from Versailles, and few have the privilege of frequent access to the gardens' splendours; yet, through the wizardry of Jean-Baptiste Leroux's photographs reproduced in this volume, the gardens are recaptured as Louis's courtiers saw them revealed, coloured and illuminated by Nature's changing moods of light and dark and animated by the King's gravity-defying caprices.

*for garden terms see Glossary p. 397

The camera has captured with surreal intensity Nature's theatrical play of light and lets us see, if only for a single instant, the full resplendent majesty of Versailles — cosmic, operatic, exhilarating and disorientating in its complexity and vastness.

Here are 'glimpses of eternity': the sun entering the palace, its temporal home, ricocheting like machine-gun fire from the windows, and bursting back onto the deserted terraces; the wind under the baroque drapery or a clouded sky churning up a tempest in the basins; the waters turned to a sea of waves under the pounding hooves of Apollo's chariot horses; the shrouding pre-dawn mist dissolving the proud and sensual marble gods and goddesses of the allées into a melancholic procession of phantoms retreating across the fields.

There is revelation in every prospect captured by the lens as it looks out from that great bulwark against the forces of Nature, the palace itself, to the panorama of the terrace where beached iron gods cavort in the tide pools of the two basins or to the ocean of the Apollo fountain and the Grand Canal, all flanked by the gardens that stretch beyond to eternity.

There is in the spiritual-sensation-seeking Romantic vision of Nature, that still informs contemporary thought, a nostalgia for the sublime, the beautiful and the picturesque. But this is not Jean-Batiste Leroux's vision of Versailles. Of course, the modern Romantic can discover the sublime in the daunting stone outcropping of Le Vau and Mansart's architecture, beauty in the flowers of the gardens and the picturesque in the artfully rusticated hamlet whose charms, for all their seductiveness, are quite unrelated to the grand theme of Versailles. However, it is the grandeur of that all-informing theme, the myth of Apollo, the Sun God, that is the theme of this collection of Leroux's striking images.

# Introduction

BAROQUE GARDEN, formal garden, French garden, Anglo-Chinese garden: so many types of garden are superimposed on each other when, after passing through the 'barrier' of the château itself, we take in at a single glance the space that contains them all as part and parcel of the allegorical perspective that is the mark of André Le Nôtre, gardener of genius, and Louis XIV, the king who commissioned the work. In fact, several centuries separate today's vision from the desires, tastes and passions of the monarchs and artists who imprinted their personalities on these gardens.

At the outset, there was wonder – wonder among Louis XIV's contemporaries at this marvel of creativity. At the outset, the monarch who fell in love with Versailles was a young man of twenty-five who found, in the meagre country house built by his father four leagues from Paris, a refuge where he could flee the constraints of court life and taste the pleasures of hunting, dance and the theatre. Some fifteen years in the 1660s and 1670s were enough for André Le Nôtre to transform this thankless and unhealthy site into a garden that would astonish the whole world. A mere fifteen years to design it, shape it, dig and fill the land; a mere fifteen years to create the grid of allées (tree-lined walks) lay out the parterres, plant entire forests, and bring into being a fairyland of water and fountains.

The *grandes eaux*, or great waters, of Versailles, in the form of still ponds, rushing streams and tumbling cascades animate the parterres, accentuate the perspectives and the interesting allées, and lend enchantment to those *salles de verdure* (clearings), enclosed by trellises and embellished with rocaille, that are known as bosquets or groves. When the waters spout, they create figures, sheaves of corn, crowns, fleurs-de-lys, or better still, they express the soul of the sculptural group that they enhance: the surging power of Apollo's chariot, the cry of pain of Enceladus struggling beneath the lava that engulfs him, the agony of a mortally wounded dragon, or the glorification of the sea-god in the Bassin (formal pond) de Neptune. Water is thus married to the magic of fables; in this case, the legend of Apollo, the sun god, with which Louis XIV (the Sun King) is identified. The most beautiful sculptures in the garden tell of the childhood of the god in the Bassin de Latone, his victory against the Python in the Bassin du Dragon, his setting out on his daily course in the Bassin d'Apollon, and his resting at the end of the day in the Grotte de Téthys, while the four Bassins des Saisons remind us that it is the sun that regulates the flow of time and life. Thus, in these fifteen years, the garden – ahead of the building of the château – established itself as the model of a royal garden. A vast garden that takes over the surrounding landscape and leads one's gaze towards the horizon. A garden made up of well-classified spaces ranging from the most artificial to the most natural: parterres, bosquets, park and forest. A garden marked out with surprising perspectives and intimate places. A garden animated not only by the play of water, but also by the movement of the shadow of carefully pruned trees projected on to sand-covered allées. A garden populated by motionless and silent statues that still convey the powerful propaganda intended by the sovereign.

In 1682, when Versailles became the official residence of the King, the court and the government, the gardens appeared finished. But, in fact, they were ceaselessly being renewed by the actions of men and of nature. The first temptation was towards excess, an excess that aimed to add even further to the *grande perspective* or great perspective which, passing through the château, follows the course of the sun from east to west over a distance of 20 kilometres (12 ½ miles). To the east, it cuts through the new town; to the west, it meets the Grand Canal, which stretches for 1,650 metres (more than a mile).

Meanwhile, under the architect Jules Hardouin-Mansart, who, after 1680, gradually supplanted Le Nôtre in royal favour, order, grandeur and richness superseded the Baroque fantasy of the garden designer. Before that, however, Le Nôtre had obtained the King's permission to make an important transformation: the creation, immediately below the château's Galerie des Glaces (completed in 1684) of the two large mirror pools of the Parterre d'Eau. It is they which, with the Grand Canal in the distance, reflect and project the ever-changing colours of the sky, passing from gentle hues of grey to violent flames of red, according to the hour, the season and the sun itself. It was also at this time that the Pièce d'Eau des Suisses was dug out, forming another of those mirrors of water that Michel Baridon, in his book *Les Jardins de Versailles*, identifies as the great novelty of the Baroque garden. Hardouin-Mansart's time was characterized by extravagance, monumentality, richness and profusion. There was the monumentality of the massive façades of the château's North and South Wings; of the new Orangerie, twice as high and as wide as its predecessor; of the two great stairways of a hundred steps; of balustrades; of constructions such as the Colonnade, for which the King sacrificed Le Nôtre's favourite Bosquet des Sources, only recently finished, with its winding paths and gentle shades. Hardouin-Mansart was the creator of this proud peristyle, where vegetation has no place, and where white marble fountains stand between the columns of coloured marble. It is marble again that triumphs in the new Trianon palace. And just as marble replaced stone, bronze replaced lead, fountains multiplied, statues proliferated and ornamental vases became gigantic. At the same time, the dialogue changed, turning from mythology to history. Apollo was no longer the inspiration. Bronze figures of the rivers and tributaries of France, reclining by the waters of the Parterre d'Eau, symbolize the excellent governance of France by the absolute monarch, while a statue of Fame writing the history of the King (known as *La Renommée du Roi*) still dominates the northern edge of the garden, beyond the Bassin de Neptune.

In a word, more display and less fantasy. But happily, the purge was not total, and one could observe in the ageing sovereign the emergence of a new taste, that of childhood, in the figures that ornamented the new fountains and bassins. And the King would conserve until his dying day the passion for his gardens. He set forth in his own hand several versions of his *Tour of the Gardens of Versailles*, all different, since he included in each revision the new projects that only ceased at his death in 1715.

As a reaction, people in the 18th century criticized the grandeur and defended unspoilt nature, which Louis XIV was accused of tyrannizing. Although this view reveals a profound lack of knowledge of Le Nôtre who, on the one hand, did his utmost to make the best of a natural site and, on the other, conceived his parterres and parks as eventually growing into great forested places, the case is closed. However, Louis XIV's successor, Louis XV, respected and even carried on the work of his great-grandfather at Versailles, endowing the Bassin of Neptune with majestic figures of marine deities. But it was at the Grand Trianon that Louis XV felt free to satisfy those tastes that he shared with his contemporaries. In place of an open meadow, he created a new domain that was at the same time private and dedicated to science and nature. In this, he was by no means at odds with the purpose that Louis XIV had previously assigned to the Grand Trianon, reserved as it was for the royal family and also being dedicated to flowers. On Louis XV's orders, the architect Ange-Jacques Gabriel first erected two pleasure pavilions, the Pavillon Français and the Salon Frais, set in a garden of relatively small proportions, with a regular layout and limited views. The King was so pleased that he ordered Gabriel to build him a new château, the

Petit Trianon. Nearby, in place of an artificial hill that dominated the small lake, he put up immense greenhouses containing four thousand plants, the largest botanical collection of the time, all methodically classified; while, in the open ground, he planted the first exotic trees, rare specimens of which still survive.

As time passed, the taste for the pseudo-natural and false simplicity grew and, with it, the fashion of the English landscape garden. This vogue risked being fatal. Although they were not in the majority, the detractors of the formal garden *à la française* spoke with a loud voice, and this at a time when the park and garden were waning. Sick from old age, trees more than a hundred years old had to be felled. Everything had to be torn up and replanted. This painful necessity coincided with the accession to the throne in 1774 of Louis XVI and, especially, the presence of Queen Marie-Antoinette, who was an enthusiast for both the natural and the picturesque. What was to be done? Restore the old model or give way to the new fashion? Already the landscape painter Hubert Robert was redesigning the Bosquet des Bains d'Apollon with its artificial grotto, as it appears today, and he also laid out the Bosquet de la Reine, a place full of charm but without the originality of the Labyrinthe, one of the splendours of Louis XIV's garden, which it replaced. These were the first steps towards a radical transformation, but happily voices were raised to convince the King to preserve the work of Le Nôtre. At the far end of the Trianon property, the gardener Claude Richard and the architect Richard Mique were able to satisfy their master without damaging the ensemble. They designed a rustic garden, set up the Temple de l'Amour, the Belvedere, and then created a village of thatched cottages, the Hameau de la Reine. After the French Revolution and the First Empire, English taste came back into fashion one final time under Louis XVIII (Louis XVI's brother), who planted the Jardin du Roi with exotic trees and shrubs of varying heights, whose contrastingly coloured foliage stands out against their surroundings.

Since the kings left Versailles, the gardens have suffered from the effects of time and weather. For more than a century, Romantic sensibility delighted in the spectacle of fallen grandeur. As nature proliferated, it reclaimed its rights, all the more so when replanting – that fatal necessity that comes round every hundred years – was interrupted by the Franco-Prussian War of 1870. People were moved by the sight of scrawny, bent, storm-stricken trees, by dilapidated bosquets and bassins in ruins, by moss-covered stones and marble, by the corrosion of bronze and lead that looked liked patination.

Finally, the 'Resurrection' of Versailles began. This undertaking was launched at the beginning of the twentieth century, but at first buildings took precedence over gardens. It was only later that people came to understand that the protection of sites lies above all in their management (as Thierry Mariage points out in his book *The World of André Le Nôtre*) and much replanting started, plot by plot, when the two great storms that marked the end of the millennium obliged the current generation of gardeners to safeguard the diversity of the estate and, where necessary, to restore the genius of Le Nôtre.

It is precisely Le Nôtre's vision that Jean-Baptiste Leroux expresses in the photographs that make up this book, in which there is a dialogue between sky and water, between the mineral and the vegetable worlds. The gardener's aim was to enchant and surprise. A victim of his success and of the pale imitations of his art that has inspired too many monotonous and boring gardens *à la française*, which can be seen in a single glance, Le Nôtre needs followers who are willing to say, 'Take your time.' Linger to watch the sun waken the statues at dawn, then draw shadows through the trellises or around the clipped yew and orange trees in planters, and finally to see it colour the Grand Canal with every nuance of a painter's palette. Take a chance and let yourself be led from the calm to the tumultuous, from the grandiose to the picturesque, from the severe to the delectable, from constraint to spontaneity – and above all, don't forget to turn around and take in every angle.

This is the invitation of Jean-Baptiste Leroux, and his records are, like those of Louis XIV, also a 'Tour of the Gardens of Versailles'. If he favours tormented skies and dramatic effects, an ambiance where atmosphere dilutes matter and shapes contours in the manner of certain great painters, he demonstrates a particular attraction for the fantastic and unusual and uses this to strengthen the effect. Thus, the terrible serpent Python seems even more frightening when wreathed in mists that evoke the pit in which he lives. There is humour and derision in the Bassin de Latone, where the frogs are gathered in mockery of the wicked peasants of Lycia who so well deserved the punishment of Jupiter. There is tenderness and sensuality in the sculpted group of Apollo Tended by Nymphs, where the photographer pays special attention to the back of one of the nymphs (who has one of the most beautiful backs ever sculpted), thus expressing the sweetness of resting at the end of the day with Tethys. But, above all, he serves the ruler of light, the god whose dawn sets the façades of the château ablaze, without forgetting his sister Diana, goddess of night, the moon whose cold rays throw a silver light on the Bassin de l'Obélisque in one of the most beautiful nocturnal views.

BEATRIX SAULE

I. 14 September, 7.45 am, the Cour de Marbre: the façades of the château are reflected in the windows of the Galerie Basse which open onto the gardens.

**2.** A winter dawn, the Bassin d'Apollon and view of the Grand Canal.

**3.** 22 March, around 8.00 am, the Bassin d'Apollon.

**4.** 13 February, 8.30 am, sunrise on the main axis of the château and the *grande perspective*.

5. 23 March, around 7.00 am, Apollo's chariot.  6. 28 January, 8.30 am.

7. 12 February, 8.45 am.  8. 25 November, 5.00 pm.

**9.** 16 August, 9.00 pm, the Bassin d'Apollon and the Grand Canal at the west end of the Tapis Vert.

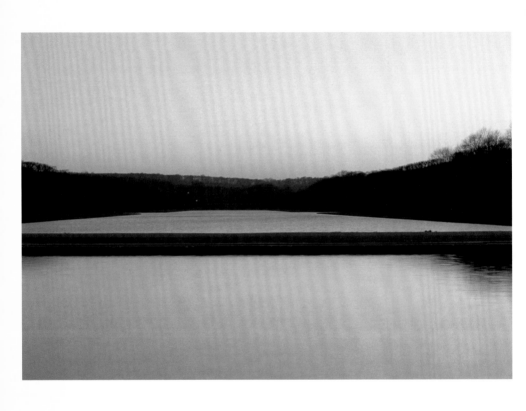

**10.** 9 December, 5.30 pm, the Bassin du Fer à Cheval and a transverse arm of the Grand Canal.

11. A March evening, around 6.30 pm, sunset over the Grand Canal…

**12.** ...and a few minutes later.

**13.** 8 July, 9.30 pm, the *grande perspective* leading up to the château.

**14.** 24 May at dusk, the *grande perspective* from the Galerie des Glaces.

**15.** A late-May morning, the Parterre du Nord seen from the Salon de la Guerre.

16. A winter dusk, the balustrade of the Parterre du Midi overlooking the Pièce d'Eau des Suisses.

**17.** 26 June, 9.15 pm, *the grande perspective.*

**18.** A winter dusk over the bassin of the Parterre du Midi.

19. A September sun sets over the Grand Canal.

**20.** Another September evening.

**21.** 8 August, around 9.00 pm, the Bassin de Latone overlooking the *grande perspective*.

22. 4 May, around 1.00 am, a storm brews over the Bassin du Fer à Cheval

**23** and **24**. 1 November, 8.10 am, the Grand Canal…

...8.30 am the same day.

25. An April morning, 7.30 am, the château seen from the Parterre d'Eau.

**26.** 23 September, 7.00 pm, the Bassin de Saturne.

**27** and **28.** 6 June, around 6.30 am, the Bassin d'Apollon.

...a few minutes later.

**29.** 12 June, 9.30 am, fountains play in the Bassin d'Apollon.

**30.** 27 August, around 4.00 pm, the Bassin d'Apollon.

**31.** A July morning, the Bassin de Cérès.

**32.** A July morning, the Bassin d'Apollon.

**33.** An April morning, 8.00 am, turning on the fountains at the Bassin d'Apollon.

**34.** 14 May, 9.30 am, the Bassin des Couronnes.

**35** and **36.** 15 May, 10.00 am, the Bassin de Latone...

... and a few minutes later.

**37.** Looking across the Bassin du Dragon up the Allée d'Eau towards the château.

**38.** 28 August, 5.20 pm, the lances of water in the Bassin de Neptune.

**39.** A May morning, fountain display in the Bassin de Neptune.

**40, 41.** A late-June morning, turning on the water at the Bassin de Neptune.

...and three minutes later.

**42.** 15 May, 10.45 am, the Bosquet des Rocailles.

**43.** 13 September, around 10.30 am, the Bassin du Fer à Cheval.

**44, 45** and **46.** 5 July, 10.00 am, the lances of water in the Bassin du Fer à Cheval…

...the changing light...

...same day, same place, in front of a transverse arm of the Grand Canal.

**47.** 5 September, 10.30 am, the Bassin du Fer à Cheval.

**48.** October 8, 3.00 pm, the Apollo Pothos statue in the Bassin du Miroir.

**49.** March 25, 7.10 pm, the château reflected in the Parterre d'Eau.

**50.** A June morning around 7.00 am, the Bassin de Latone.

**51.** 18 June, 7.00 pm, the Orangerie and château seen from the Pièce d'Eau des Suisses.

**52.** 11 February, around 10.15 am, ornamental vase in the Bassin de Neptune.

**53.** A late-winter morning at the Trianon Belvedere, the Pavillon de Musique and Rocher.

**54.** A winter morning at the Grand Trianon.

**55.** An autumn afternoon at the Bassin du Miroir.

**56.** 15 October, 8.30 am, the Parterre d'Eau.

**57.** Late afternoon in May, the Crouching Venus.

58, 59. An autumn afternoon, a marble fountain in the Salle des Marronniers.

**60.** 12 October, 4.00 pm, the Bosquet de l'Encelade.

**61.** Mid-August, around 4.00 pm, the Bosquet de l'Obélisque.

**62.** 30 August, between 4.30 and 5.00 pm, the pool in the Bosquet de l'Obélisque.

**63.** 6 October, 3.30 pm, the Bosquet des Dômes.

**64** and **65**. April, 7.00 am, the Cabinet du Combat des Animaux in the Parterre du Nord.

...and at 7.10 am, the Cabinet du Combat des Animaux in the Parterre du Midi.

**66, 67, 68** and **69.** A July morning, around 8.00 am, orange trees in the Parterre de Latone.

...A July morning, around 8.00 am...

...a September morning, around 8.00 am.

**70.** I July, 7.15 am, the *grande perspective*.

**71.** 5 September, 7.30 am, an orange tree in the Parterre de Latone.

**72.** A Spring evening around 8.00 pm, statue of the Dordogne in the Parterre d'Eau.

**73.** The Fontaine des Lézards in the Parterre de Latone.

**74.** 15 October, 7.30 am, the Hameau de la Reine.

**75.** An October morning, around 9.45 am, the Trianon-sous-Bois staircase in the Grand Trianon.

**76.** 1 November, 9.20 am, the surroundings of the Etoile Royale.

77. 15 September, 9.00 am, Cyparissus and his deer.

**78.** Late morning in November, shadow of Bacchus near the Bassin d'Apollon.

**79.** An October morning, 10.30 am, bacchante in the Parterre de Latone.

**80.** 9 September, around 7.00 pm, Ino and Melicertes.

**81** and **82**. An afternoon in late August, Ino and Melicertes.

...under the full moon, 5 July.

**83.** A summer morning, Bosquet de la Colonnade.

**84.** The marble group of the Rape of Proserpine.

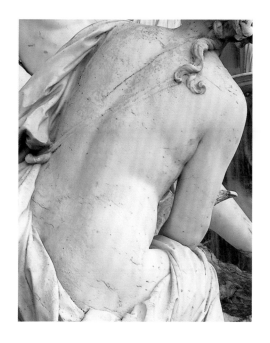

**Detail of 85.** Apollo Tended by Nymphs.

**85.** A July afternoon, around 5.45 pm, the group of Apollo Tended by Nymphs in the Bosquet des Bains d'Apollon.

**86.** 15 July, 7.00 pm, the Horses of the Sun in the Bosquet des Bains d'Apollon.

**87.** 13 July, 6.30 pm, the Bosquet des Bains d'Apollon.

**88.** 12 July, 6.30 pm, the Bassin du Fer à Cheval.

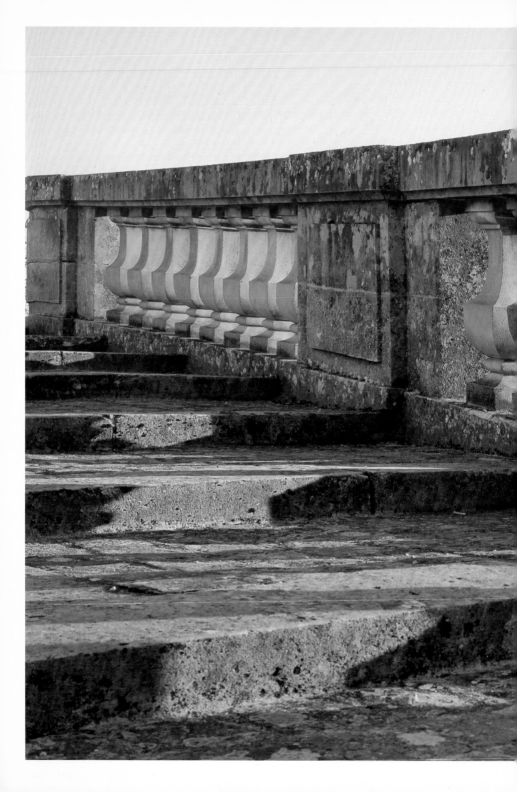

**89.** A winter morning at the Bassin du Fer à Cheval.

**90.** A winter morning at the Grand Trianon, the Fer à Cheval steps and the Grand Canal.

**91** and **92.** 26 November, 4.00 pm, the Grand Canal seen from the balustrade of the Grand Trianon.

... 24 April at 4.00 pm.

**93.** 14 June in the afternoon, the Grand Trianon and Grand Canal.

**94.** 15 March, late afternoon at the Grand Trianon.

**95.** 15 February, 10.15 am, overlooking the Bosquet de la Reine from the Orangerie.

**96.** 15 February, 9.50 am, on the Cent Marches staircase.

**97.** 15 February, 10.40 am, steps in the Parterre du Midi

**98.** 15 February, 9.40 am, the Bassin de l'Orangerie.

**99, 100, 101** and **102.** 24 June, 6.30 pm, the shaped turf in the Parterre de l'Orangerie.

...a few minutes later.

**103.** 12 July, 10.30 am, flower beds, fountains and clipped yew in the Parterre de Latone.

**104** and **105.** 24 April, 9.00 am, *broderie* pattern of clipped box and yew in the Parterre du Midi…

...and the following day, view with potted orange trees.

106. The Parterre du Midi in bloom, 3 April, 7.40 pm.

**107.** The Parterre du Midi seen from the Grands Appartements.

**108.** 25 April, 7.30 am, the Parterre du Nord.

**109.** 26 July, 7.00 am, the Parterre de Latone.

110. A spring morning in the Jardin du Roi.

III. A summer afternoon, allée leading to the Jardin du Roi.

112 and 113. 25 May, 8.30 am, Allée des Trois Fontaines.

114 and 115. 3 April, 8.15 pm, the *grande perspective* towards the Grand Canal, from the Bassin de Latone...

...and at 8.35 pm.

116 and 117. A September afternoon, linden trees long the Grand Canal

...and in late January.

**118.** 1 November, 9.30 am, at the end of the Grand Canal, the surroundings of the Etoile Royale.

**119.** 1 November, 7.45 am, sunrise on the Grand Canal.

**120** and **121**. 1 November, 8.10 am, on the Grand Canal...

...and at 8.45 am.

122. A late-October morning, the Grand Canal with the château in the distance.

**123** and **124**. I November, 8.45 am, the château seen from the Grand Canal...

...and a little later on.

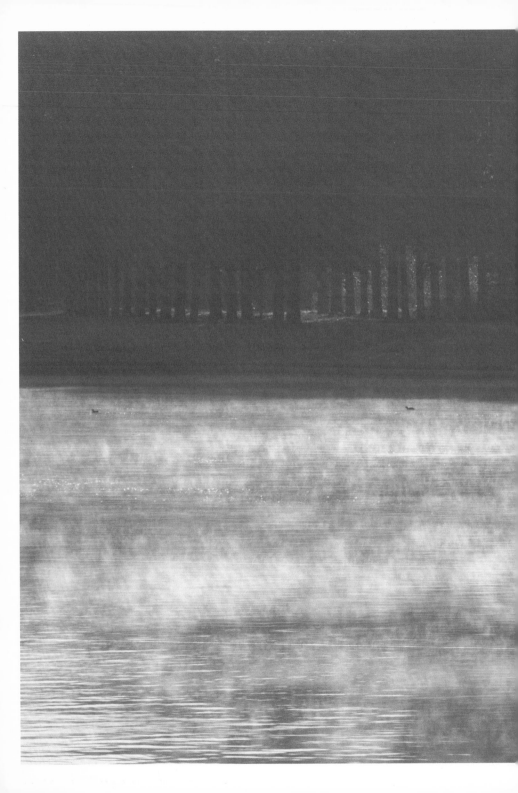

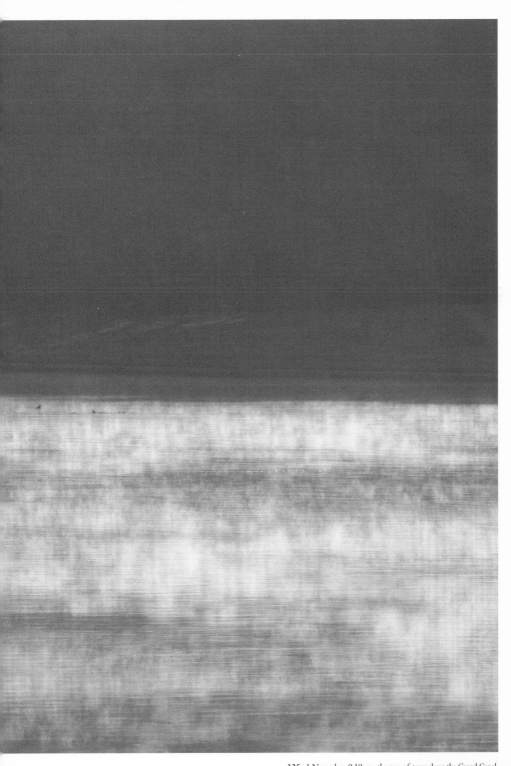

**125.** 1 November, 9.10 am, the row of trees along the Grand Canal.

126 and 127. 4 May, 8.00 am, statue of Neptune and Amphritite in the Bassin de Neptune...

...and later in the day, statue of Oceanus.

**128** and **129.**  4 May, 8.30 am, statue of a child riding a swan in the Bassin du Dragon…

...the same scene a few minutes later.

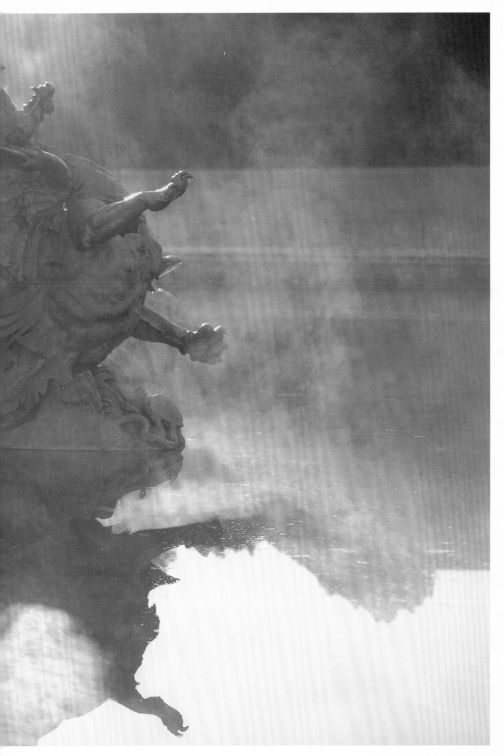

**130.** 4 May, 8.50 am, the Bassin du Dragon.

**131.** 13 July, 8.30 am, the Bassin du Dragon.

132. A June morning, dolphin and horses in the Bassin d'Apollon

**133.** A September morning, 9.30 am, frogs in the Bassin de Latone.

**134.** 14 August, 8.30 am, the Bassin du Dragon.

**135.** An April morning, 8.30 am, the Cabinet du Combat des Animaux in the Parterre du Nord

**136.** An April morning, 8.45 am, the Cabinet du Combat des Animaux in the Parterre du Nord.

**137, 138** and **139.** An April morning, 8.50 am, ornamental trophies on the parapet of the château…

...and at 8.55 am.

**140** and **141**.  9 September, 6.00 pm, Laocoön and his sons near the Parterre de Latone...

...and at 8.30 pm.

**142.** An April morning, 7.45 am, the château seen from the Parterre d'Eau.

**143.** A July evening, the Loiret in the Parterre d'Eau.

**144.** 12 May, 9.45 am, statue of Ino and Melicertes near the Bassin d'Apollon.

**145.** 13 July, 9.30 pm, figure of Daybreak in the Parterre d'Eau.

**146** and **147**. 14 June, 6.00 am, sunlight streams into the Galerie Basse...

...and the château seen from the gardens.

**148.** 14 June, 6.10 am, the statue of the Marne in the Parterre d'Eau.

**149.** A September morning, 9.50 am, detail from the Bains des Nymphes de Diane.

**150.** A September morning, 9.55 am, detail from the Bains des Nymphes de Diane in the Allée d'Eau.

**151.** Late afternoon in autumn, bust of Marcus Aurelius in the Salle des Marroniers.

**152.** A June morning, Pomona and Bacchus around the Bassin d'Apollon.

153. An afternoon in May, 5.00 pm, Bacchus in the Allée d'Apollon.

**154.** An afternoon in May, 5.00 pm, statue of Light in the Allée d'Apollon.

**155.** A September morning around 9.00 am, statue of the Choleric in an allée of the Parterre du Nord

**156.** A September afternoon, Ceres in front of the Bassin de Cérès.

**157.** 24 April, 9.30 am, steps of the Parterre de Latone.

158. A June evening at the Bassin des Couronnes in the Parterre du Nord.

**159** and **160.** 15 February, 9.00 am, the Temple de l'Amour at the Petit Trianon...

...late morning in autumn, Cupid carving a bow from Hercules' club.

**161.** 10 November, 10.15 am, Fame writing the history of the King, near the Bassin de Neptune.

**162.** 12 April, 10.30 am, nymph with a shell in the Parterre de Latone.

**163.** 6 June, 8.45 pm, Spring and Bacchus border the Bassin d'Apollon.

**164** and **165.** The Parterre d'Eau in May, group depicting a child with a bird...

...and a little later, statue of the Marne.

**166.** An October dawn, detail of the group with dolphins in the Parterre d'Eau.

**167** and **168.** A morning and afternoon in May, fountains with children (or Marmousets).

**169.** A late-October morning, the Bassin de l'Ile des Enfants.

**170.** 30 May, 6.00 pm, the Bosquet de l'Encelade.

**171.** A July evening, the Ceres and Flora bassins.

**172.** 20 April, 6.45 pm, the Jardin du Roi.

173 and 174. Winter and autumn dusk at the Bassin de Bacchus.

**175.** The Bassin de Flore on a late-winter morning.

176, 177 and 178. Morning view of the Bassin de Cérès, in February, April and July.

179. 17 August, 7.30 pm, the Allée d'Apollon.

**180.** The Bassin de Saturne, 3 June, 9.30 am.

**181.** 10 September, 8.30 am, the Bassin de Saturne.

**182.** 15 June, 10.30 am, at the foot the Cent Marches staircase

**183.** 6 May, 8.45 am, ornamental vases at the Bassin de Neptune.

**184.** A July morning around 11.00 am, garden front of the Grand Trianon.

**185** and **186.**  15 March, 4.30 pm, peristyle of the Grand Trianon...

...and on 15 September.

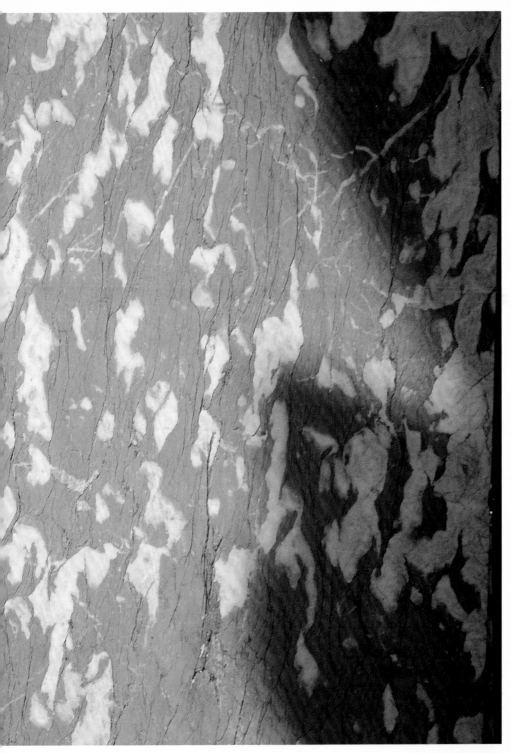

187, 188 and 189. An afternoon in late August, in the Bosquet de la Colonnade.

190. An afternoon in late August, pleached trees and trelliswork.

**191.** 6 October, 4.15 pm, the Bosquet de l'Encelade.

**192.** 18 July, 6.00 pm, term of Minerva in the Bosquet de la Girandole.

**193.** 8 October, 4.30 pm, the Bosquet des Dômes.

**194.** A September morning, around 11.00 am, the Bosquet de la Girandole.

**195.** 13 May, 5.30 pm, statue of Liberality in the Bosquet du Dauphin.

**196.** An October afternoon in the Salle des Marronniers.

**197.** 24 April, 9.00 am, the Jardin Anglais at the Petit Trianon.

**198.** An October morning, the Bassin du Plat-Fond at the Grand Trianon.

**199** and **200**.  12 July, 5.30 pm, the Bassin des Nymphes in the Amphithéâtre d'Alexandre, Grand Trianon…

...and on a winter morning.

**201**. An April morning, statues surrounding the Bassin d'Apollon.

**202.** An April morning, the Bassin d'Apollon.

**203.** A winter dusk on the Grand Canal.

**204** and **205**.  24 October, 9.00 am, the Allée d'Apollon...

...and on 14 August, 7.15 pm.

**206.** An autumn morning, Apollo on his chariot.

**207.** 1 November, 10.30 am, the Allée d'Apollon.

**208.** 30 October, 2.30 pm, the Bosquet de la Reine.

**209.** Early afternoon in autumn, an allée flanking the Tapis Vert.

**210.** 12 October, 9.40 am, the Trianon-sous-Bois wing of the Grand Trianon.

**211.** I November, 8.45 am, the Etoile Royale.

**212.** 1 November, 10.30 am, a paved allée at Trianon.

**213.** An October morning, around 9.00 am, open fields behind the Grand Trianon.

**214.** 8 July, 9.30 pm, view of the château from the Grand Canal.

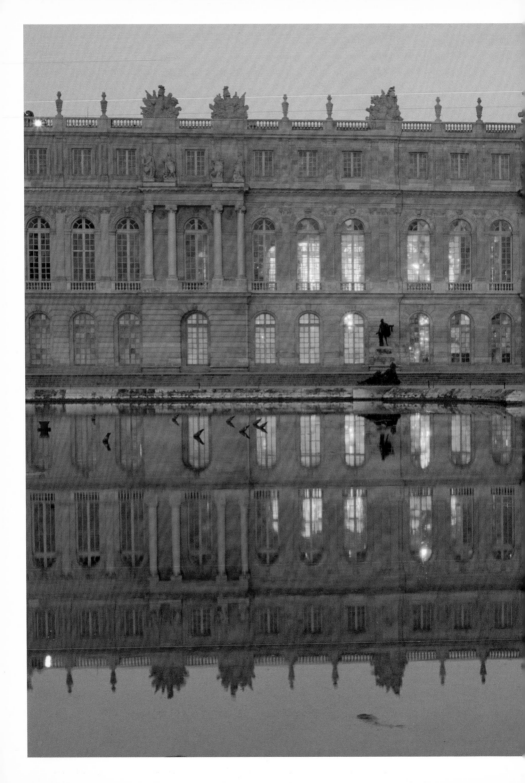

**215.** An evening in March, around 5.00 pm, the château is lit up by the rays of the sun setting over the Grand Canal.

**216, 217** and **218, 219.** 10 August, 8.45 pm, in front of the façade, the Apollo Belvedere and the figure of the Dordogne in the Parterre d'Eau...

...at 8.50 pm...

…and at 8.55 pm.

# Appendix

As with all chroniclers, Jean-Baptiste Leroux has withheld his personal opinion. The aim of the following pages is to provide a historical, topographical and aesthetic background, with which we did not wish to distract the reader in the previous pages.

# Chronology
## 1623–1668

1623: Louis XIII, 'the melancholy king', comes to hunt on this modest estate and builds a small château for himself and close friends. In 1627, the first bosquet is laid out and in 1631, after acquiring some twenty acres, a kitchen garden, an orchard and a holly grove are added and this area becomes known as the Bois Vert (green wood) until Louis XIV's reign. In 1633 the first water pump is installed to feed the fountain in the parterre, while two gardeners, Jacques Boyceau and Jacques de Menours, begin laying out the parterres and garden; additional land is acquired to endow the property with a park.

1638: Louis, Dauphin of France and the future King Louis XIV, is born in Saint-Germain-en-Laye.

1643–52: Louis XIII dies and a period of regency begins during which Queen Anne of Austria, her minister Cardinal Mazarin and the young King Louis XIV, are forced to confront the Fronde (1648–53), a series of revolts by Parliament, the high nobility and the people against the growing authority of the Crown and heavy taxation. The uprising, which obliged the King to flee Paris for Saint-Germain, would explain, according to some historians, the King's aversion to the capital.

1656: Nicolas Fouquet, the King's Finance minister, entrusts André Le Nôtre – since 1643 the 'designer of plans and parterres of all His Majesty's gardens' – with the layout of his own gardens at the château of Vaux-le-Vicomte.

1660: In June, Louis XIV marries Maria Teresa of Austria, the Spanish Infanta, and takes her to Versailles on 25 October.

1661: After the death of Cardinal Mazarin, the young sovereign declares that he will rule his kingdom alone and appoints Jean-Baptiste Colbert as head of Finance. Great festivities take place at Vaux-le-Vicomte, where Fouquet receives the King and his court, precipitating his fall from power; Fouquet is arrested a few weeks later. During this same year, which sees the birth of the Dauphin of France on November 1, Mademoiselle de La Vallière gains the King's favour, and the two often hunt together at Versailles. He hands over the small kitchen garden to Jean-Baptiste de la Quintinie, an expert gardener who carries out botanical experiments there.

1662: A decision is made to renovate the small château built by Louis XIII. Louis XIV orders the architect Louis Le Vau to redesign the rooms and places André Le Nôtre in charge of the gardens. This marks the beginning of a long-lasting co-operation and friendship between the young, twenty-four-year-old monarch and the fifty-year-old gardener. It is also the first step in a landscaping programme of unrivalled grandeur and scale, in which the scientific knowledge of the time is used to level and shape the terrain, to create terraces, perspectives, allées and woodland that will consume entire forests brought from all over France. Thousands of rare flowers

are introduced into Paris for the Jardin du Roi, along with mineral and vegetable sculptures.

1663: The court resides at Versailles for the first time (October 13–22). The Orangerie, designed to shelter the collection of exotic trees in winter, is built by Louis Le Vau below the Parterre du Midi, then known as the Parterre de l'Amour or the Parterre des Fleurs; further to the south-west, the Ménagerie, housing rare and exotic animals, is completed and fountains are added; to the north of the château, the future Bassin du Dragon is excavated and a water tower and three reservoirs are installed to feed the fountains.

1664: May 7–13, Louis XIV brings the entire court to Versailles for a court festivity or *fête* entitled *Les Plaisirs de l'Isle Enchantée*. For the first time in his reign, such an entertainment does not take place in Paris – as was the case in 1662 with the magnificent Carrousel which gave a crowd of ten thousand people the opportunity to see the Sun King in all his splendour as a horseman and dancer – but in the gardens of Versailles, which are transformed into a theatre by Charles Vigarani. For seven days a series of jousting, tilting at the ring, chariot processions, performances by Lully and Molière takes place, reaching a climax with the destruction of the palace of Alcina, a sorceress who was holding prisoner the valiant Ruggiero – played by the King – and his knights. The historiographer André Félibien's description of this event, illustrated with engravings by Israël Silvestre, manifests to the rest of Europe the importance that the King attaches to this place dedicated to his pleasure.

1665–68: Despite opposition from Jean-Baptiste Colbert, who in 1664 was appointed Surintendant des Bâtiments (supervising buildings and by extension the gardens), and then Contrôleur Général des Finances in 1665, Louis XIV continues to spend money on the château and gardens of Versailles. The vast Parterre du Nord had by then already been laid out in its present form. The Grotte de Thétys is built beneath a reservoir and ornamented, among other things, with the sculptural group of Apollo Tended by Nymphs, a marble masterpiece by François Girardon and Thomas Regnaudin, as well as by two groups of the Horses of the Sun by Gilles Guérin and the Marsy brothers, Balthazar and Gaspard. The first statues and stone terms are erected in the gardens.

In 1666, south of the main east-west axis, work begins on the Bosquet du Labyrinthe (inspired by Charles Perrault) and the site is endowed with thirty-nine lead fountains depicting Aesop's fables.

While the King continues to make Saint-Germain-en-Laye, rather than the Louvre, his main residence, the first opening ceremonies for the *grandes eaux* take place at Versailles, the Allée d'Eau is laid out and decorated with fountains designed by Charles Le Brun (named Court Painter in 1662), and endless new building projects begin, the Bassin du Fer à Cheval, the Bassin de Latone and the two Bassins des Lézards, but most importantly, the Bassin d'Apollon, to which will be added Jean-Baptiste Tuby's sculpture.

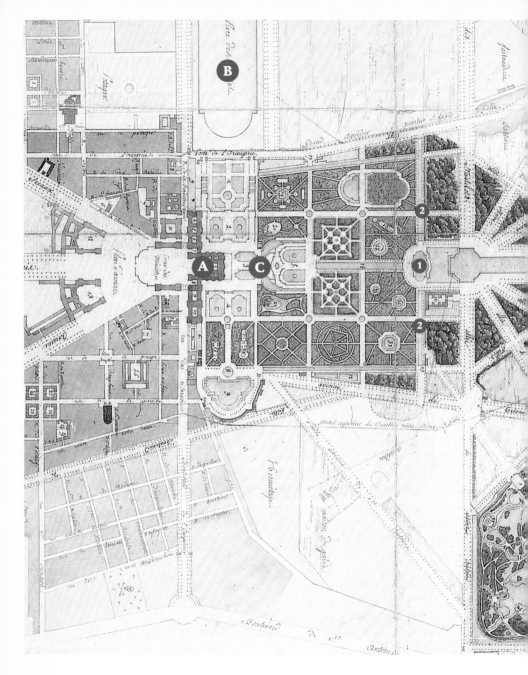

THE ESTATE OF VERSAILLES

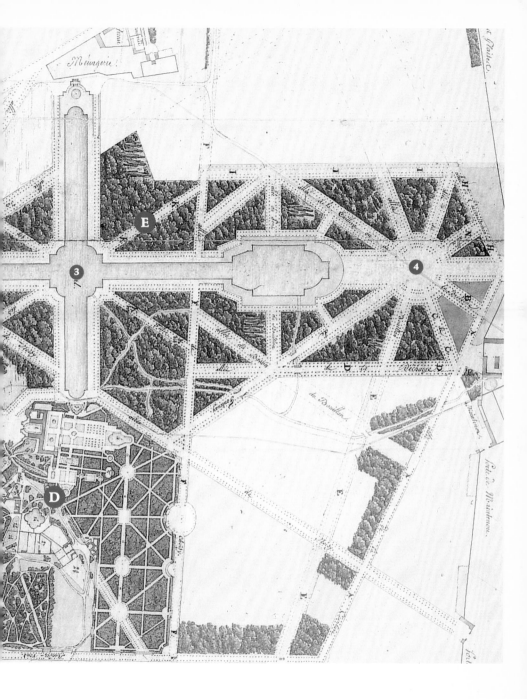

A - CHÂTEAU

B - PIÈCE D'EAU DES SUISSES

C - GARDENS

D - TRIANON

E - PARK

  1 - BASSIN D'APOLLON

  2 - ALLÉE D'APOLLON

  3 - GRAND CANAL

  4 - ÉTOILE ROYALE

# THE GARDENS

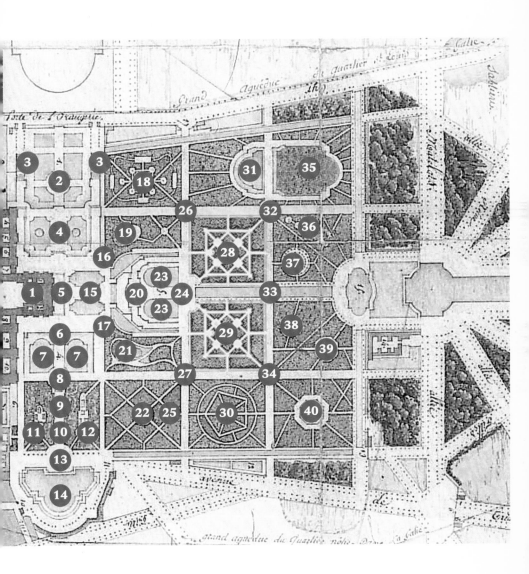

# TRIANON

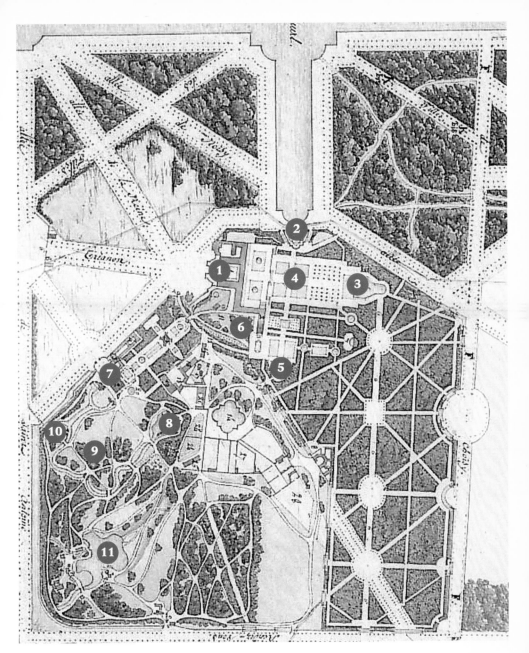

# Chronology
## 1668–2002

1668: Louis XIV, who had invaded the Netherlands in May 1667, victoriously enters Franche-Comté, and signs the peace treaty of Aix-La-Chapelle on May 2, 1668. A celebration, the *Grand Divertissement Royal*, is held in honour of his military success on July 18 in the gardens of Versailles. The festivities also celebrate the triumph of the King's new favourite, Madame de Montespan, over Mademoiselle de la Vallière. The event, which sees refreshments and a comédie-ballet, lasts from sunset to sunrise and ends with firework displays, all staged in delicate settings, which are preserved in the account of Félibien and the engravings of Jean Le Pautre. The same year a proposal is passed to enlarge Louis XIII's château and, after much hesitation, Louis Le Vau is entrusted with the task of building a solid 'envelope' around this 'small château of cards'. In the gardens, construction begins on the Bosquet du Dauphin and the Bosquet de la Girandole, already laid out, in the Parterre du Nord, on the Bassin de la Pyramide, the Bassin des Couronnes and the Bassin des Nymphes de Diane, which features a relief by François Girardon.

Excavation and construction work also begins on the Grand Canal, which is completed 1670.

1669–73: After the death of Louis Le Vau in 1670, the architect François d'Orbay builds the *grands appartments* of the King and Queen, private bosquets are framed in trelliswork, the main allées and flanking allées are lined with trees and punctuated with fountains. Madame de Montespan – for whom the King built the Trianon de Porcelaine in 1670 – suggests the idea for the Bosquet du Marais, and Le Nôtre's work continues at a brisk pace. He designs the northern bosquets, the *pavillon d'eau* (water arbour) the *berceau d'eau* (water bower), and the Salle des Festins (or Salle du Conseil); he orders the excavation of the Ile Royale and the four Bassins des Saisons. In front of the château a new Parterre d'Eau is designed by Charles Le Brun around the iconography of Apollo. In 1671 the Grand Canal reaches 1,650 metres in length, and two long transverse arms lead southwards to the Ménagerie and northwards to Trianon.

1674: The reconquest of Franche-Comté by Louis XIV is marked by the another great *fête*, the *Divertissements de Versailles donnés par le roi à toute sa cour* ('amusements at Versailles provided by the king to the whole court') again described by Félibien and engraved by Le Pautre. Six days of festivities are held between 4 July and 31 August, and magical settings are created throughout the gardens. The celebration opens with refreshments in the Bosquet du Marais, followed, in the Cour de Marbre, by a performance of *Alceste* staged by Vigarani. On the second day a 'leafy bower shaped like a salon and decorated with flowers' is set up in the gardens of the Trianon de Porcelaine for a concert, which is followed by supper in the Bosquet des Festins. On the third day, after refreshments are served at the Ménagerie, the Grotte de Thétys provides the scenery for Molière's *Malade Imaginaire*, presented a year after the playwright's death. Le Nôtre and François Francine, 'the fountain maker', design the settings for the fourth day of festivities on 28 July. Refreshments in the Bosquet du Théâtre d'Eau are followed by a ballet by the Bassin du Dragon and finally a *medianoche* (midnight) supper in the illuminated Cour de Marbre. The Grand Canal is the undisputed star of the two last days, 18 and 31 August. On 18 August, the King is presented with conquered flags and supper is given; then follows a fireworks display organized by Le Brun at the head of the Grand Canal, which features an obelisk crowned by the sun. The *Divertissements* are closed with celebrations in the night of 31 August; the King and his court embark on a musical pleasure-trip on the Grand Canal, decorated the entire length with illuminated sculptures 'of palaces, pyramids, fountains, figures, terms, fish…'.

This year is also marked by the *grande commande* (great commission), for which Colbert asks Le Brun to design a set of statues for the Parterre d'Eau. Twenty-four pieces are sculpted for the four bassins, and divided into six themes of four statues each: the four Elements, the four Seasons, the four Times of Day, the four Continents – all governed by the sun, symbol of the King – the four Humours of Man and the four kinds of Poetry. To these are added four large 'abduction' groups.

1675–76: The growing number of bassins, fountains and large pieces of ornamental water entails a constant search for new water sources. In 1765 the King buys the property of Glatigny to install a great reservoir there. In the same year, decorated with the Ordre du Saint-Esprit and ennobled, Le Nôtre creates the Bosquet de l'Encelade and Bosquet de la Renommée, which, a year later, Jules Hardouin-Mansart – newly appointed to Versailles – plans to transform into the Bosquet des Dômes.

1677: A significant date, as Louis XIV declares his intention to make Versailles his official residence. It will now become, if not the capital of France, at least the centre of the kingdom.

The *berceau d'eau* on one side of the Allée d'Eau becomes the Bosquet des Trois Fontaines and the *pavillon d'eau* on the other side becomes the Bosquet de l'Arc de Triomphe.

1678: Louis XIV is forty, André Le Nôtre sixty-five, and Jules Hardouin-Mansart forty-two. Following the King's wishes, Hardouin-Mansart undertakes new building work: the terrace of the château overlooking the gardens is replaced by the Grande Galerie or Galerie des Glaces (completed 1684), and the South Wing is built (completed 1683). In the gardens, construction begins on the new Orangerie (completed 1688), a vast cathedral-like space where the theories of Jean-Baptiste de La Quintinie (for protecting exotic trees against frost without artificial heating) are applied. The north-south axis of the gardens is prolonged by a stretch of water, the Pièce d'Eau des Suisses, named after the Swiss regiment that excavated it. La Quintinie takes advantage of the alterations to plant the Nouveau Potager du Roi, a kitchen garden to provide the royal table with fruit and vegetables, in particular early vegetables.

1679–81: While André Le Nôtre is on a three-month trip to Italy, the Nassau regiment spends over seventy days planting large trees in the park. In 1680 the central strip of the Allée

Royale is covered in turf and becomes known as the Tapis Vert (green carpet). On his return, Le Nôtre orders excavation work to begin at the end of the Allée d'Eau for the Bassin de Neptune, which will be endowed with vases and sculptures on the theme of sea gods. He also creates the Bosquet des Rocailles (completed 1683) and the Bosquet des Sources, his favourite. Hardouin-Mansart starts work on the Grande and Petite Ecurie (grand and lesser stables), which are finished in 1682.

1682: On 6 May, the King, court and government are established at Versailles. Construction starts on the Grand Commun (to be finished in 1684) as well as the gigantic, monstrously noisy and relatively inefficient *machine de Marly*, a pumping station intended to fill the reservoirs with water drawn from the Seine.

1683: The Parterre d'Eau in front of the Galerie des Glaces (near completion), no longer suits the King's taste, as the statues impede the first-floor view, which should stretch to the horizon along the east-west axis. His idea, his grand idea, is to clear the central axis of any obstacles and to achieve this, the original bassins are replaced by two rectangular pieces of water. The marble rims are decorated with horizontal figures, bronze is used instead of gilded lead and allegories of the rivers and tributaries of France are preferred to the theme of Apollo. To complete the parterre before the steps that lead to the Bassin de Latone, two fountains on the north and south side form the Cabinets du Combat des Animaux. The twenty-four marble figures originally created for the parterre are distributed throughout the gardens and bosquets, casually mixed with antique statues, copies of antiques, works of the period and terms which Fouquet had commissioned for Vaux-le-Vicomte, but were subsequently bought by the King.

1684–1700: The gardens, like the château, are open to all, in accordance with the wishes of the King 'whose duty is to his people', and become a place for power games, display and etiquette. As with the King's movements inside the château, not all may follow him in his walks along the allées, during which he notices the smallest details and the smallest failures in the carrying out of his orders. Apart from the Doge of Genoa in 1685 and the ambassadors of Siam in 1686, who are granted the privilege of a guided tour by the sovereign himself, most grand visitors follow the itinerary fixed by Louis XIV in his *Manière de montrer les jardins de Versailles* (Tour of the Gardens of Versailles), the first version appearing in 1689. Visitors around this time no longer find the original Grotte of Thétys, which is destroyed at the end of 1684, but they can see the latest innovations and transformations. The Bosquet de la Colonnade, built by Hardouin-Mansart in 1684, is not the least of these projects, and favours stone over greenery, in what Le Nôtre called 'a mason's work', according to the Duc de Saint-Simon, a noble at the court. Though the bosquets are occasionally closed to avoid them being plundered, they nevertheless serve as outdoor salons for resident courtiers, whose

pastimes include sledging or skating on the Grand Canal in winter and, when fair weather returns, playing pall-mall or other such destructive games in the covered paths of the Bosquet de l'Encelade.

The King, Madame de Maintenon (whom he secretly married in 1683) and the royal family, including those children declared legitimate (despite their mother, Madame de Montespan, having left the court in 1685), enjoy the privacy of the Trianon de Marbre built by Hardouin-Mansart between 1687 and 1688. This replaced the earlier Trianon de Porcelaine, but retains the name of the Palais de Flore, and here 'good Monsieur Le Nôtre' re-creates the Bosquet des Sources, which he cherishes the most among his works, perhaps because he saw old age approaching. This awareness seems confirmed in the gift he made to the King of a large part of his valuable painting collection in 1693.

The King finds at the Château de Marly an even greater relief from the etiquette of court life. Designed by Hardouin-Mansart, this 'hermitage' with its central building surrounded by twelve pavilions for specially chosen guests, is a place of ceaseless creativity, particularly in the art of topiary.

1700–15: At sixty-two, undoubtedly feeling his age, the King still holds passionately to the exercise of power and to his gardens. On 16 November, 1700, he accepts, in the name of his grandson, the Duc d'Anjou, the *Succession de toutes les Espagnes* (succession to the Spanish throne), knowing that it brings with it the threat of an enemy coalition, which happens in 1701. Le Nôtre dies on 15 September, 1700, ten years after Le Brun. Hardouin-Mansart is now all-powerful in the King's service. In 1700 he has the Rape of Prosperine, originally commissioned from Girardon for the Parterre d'Eau, placed in 'his' Colonnade; he extends the garden at Trianon towards the north-west with salles and bosquets surrounded by blocks of triangular-shaped woodland and creates the *buffet d'eau*. In 1704 he replaces the Galerie des Antiques, designed by Le Nôtre in 1680, with the Salle des Marronniers; the Bosquet du Marais is destroyed in favour of a new arrangement in which the three sculptural groups commissioned for the Grotte de Thétys are installed under gilded canopies; the same year, rows of majestic sweet chestnuts are planted along the Tapis Vert, enhancing the perspective. In 1705 the allée surrounding the Bassin d'Apollon to the east is widened into a semi-circle, creating a vast sanded esplanade between the bassin and the Grand Canal. In 1706 Hardouin-Mansart removes the trellises and scented plants from the Bosquet de l'Encelade, along with the shrubs in gilded vases and even the rocaille fountains, only keeping the central bassin.

By the end of Louis XIV's reign, only one construction project is still underway, the Chapel Royal, completed in 1710 by Robert de Cotte; its tall roof bristling with sculptures towers over the Parterre du Nord. With war, Hardouin-Mansart's death in 1708 and several losses within the royal family – which, on the death of Louis XIV in 1715 only leaves a five-year-old great-grandson as successor – the gardens are now more a place for reflection than change.

### In Search of Pleasure

1715–21: During the regency, the princes and court leave for Paris and the young Louis XV moves to the Tuileries palace after a brief stay at the château of Vincennes. In Paris, 1721, he receives the young Spanish Infanta whom he is to marry when she comes of age. In the vast empty property of Versailles, nature, 'enslaved' by Louis XIV, is still kept under control; flower beds, carefully clipped yew, pleached hedges, fountains and waterworks are all maintained in working condition and the garden appears to have reached maturity.

1722–41: Louis XV is twelve years old when he rediscovers Versailles on 15 June, 1722. The young Infanta joins him there for a brief period, but is sent back to Spain in 1725 so the King can marry Maria Leczinska, an older Polish princess. The gardens are only altered by time, with the exception of the Bassin de Neptune, which is almost entirely rebuilt by the architect Ange-Jacques Gabriel, nearly a century after it was designed by Le Nôtre. The lead sculptures of allegories and sea monsters are created between 1738 and 1741 by the sculptors Lambert-Sigisberg Adam, Edme Bouchardon and Jean-Baptiste Lemoyne.

1742–53: Having little inclination to make major changes, Louis XV, 'the beloved king', concentrates on creating intimate spaces, both inside and outside the château, and he hosts dinners in private rooms after a day's hunting – his passion. From 1745, Madame de Pompadour shines at these dinners, alleviating the King's boredom, and she soon directs his attention to Trianon, a small four-acre estate, ideally secluded. A Ménagerie is built, quite different from the one that Louis XIV commissioned for the end of the southern arm of the Grand Canal, as the new Ménagerie houses nothing exotic, but is used to rear and create new breeds of cattle and birds. Set up by Gabriel to the north-east of the château of Trianon, the Ménagerie is completed with a classical garden of symmetrical layout, which nevertheless displays two overlapping circular allées and a small maze with clearings.

Gabriel's elegant Pavillon Français (built 1749–50) on the axis of the Ménagerie is used for entertaining and games. It is completed in 1753 with the Salon Frais to the west, which functions as a dining room where produce from the dairy and kitchen garden is served.

1762–66: Gabriel's new buildings at Trianon signal, more than any other project, a return to neo-classical taste after the delightful extravagance of rocaille. They feature a square plan with four different façades inspired by ancient Greece, which open out onto four different perspectives. The courtyard faces south, an ornamental garden to the west stretches towards the Pavillon Français with the Ménagerie and Salon Frais on either side; this garden becomes known as the Jardin Français from 1774, as opposed to the Jardin Anglais which is created at the same time; to the north and east lies a rigorous square grid designed to display Bernard de Jussieu's plant collection. Developed and enriched with small greenhouses and a large 'Dutch' hothouse for tropical plants,

this Jardin Botanique rapidly becomes one of the most famous botanical gardens in Europe.

1770–74: Aged 60, Louis XV – no longer known as 'the beloved king' in a kingdom stirred by the spirit of the Enlightenment – celebrates with great pomp the marriage of his grandson the Dauphin to Marie-Antoinette, Archduchess of Austria. Gabriel's new opera house is inaugurated and thanks to his ingenious design, it can also be converted into a banquet hall. In the gardens the trees planted by Louis XIV are lit up for what is to be the last time. Even though Louis XV agrees to have eight thousand trees replanted in 1747, he refuses, right up to his death on 10 May, 1774, to give into Gabriel's suggestion to remodel the bosquets.

### The King at Versailles, the Queen at Trianon

1774–76: As soon as he comes to power, the young Louis XVI gives the Trianon property to his eighteen-year-old queen, while he concentrates on repairing the damage caused to Versailles by the weather and the passage of time. Two winters are spent felling the ancient trees and studying projects that contradict each other in their outline and essence; how could one not be tempted by the fashionable Anglo-Chinese taste and new, exotic plant species from distant lands?

And what of loyalty and thrift? Le Nôtre's general design is kept in the gardens, and the trees and plants are mostly sourced from French nurseries. However, Michel Hazon, the Intendant des Bâtiments in charge of the gardens, plans more diagonal allées and the destruction of the Bosquet du Dauphin and de la Girandole, which are replaced by the Quinconce du Nord and du Midi, shaded by linden trees and sweet chestnut. Other bosquets, such as the Bosquet de l'Arc de Triomphe and the Théâtre d'Eau, are neglected, while others are radically remodelled in a more modern style. The Bosquet du Labyrinthe with its fables represented in lead sculpture, later becomes the Bosquet de la Reine, and cedars of Lebanon, Corsican pines and Virginia tulip poplars are planted

within its winding paths. The Bosquet des Bains d'Apollon is the next to be remodelled, but Hazon's designs and the plans of the architect Richard Mique are not carried out.

1777–89: The Queen retains her property at Trianon for her friends, and decorates it according to her taste for the 'naturalistic' and the 'picturesque' garden. She stays more frequently and important work is carried out in the grounds; between 1774 and 1783, an English garden replaces the botanical garden with its Dutch hothouse, a small lake is built and embankments are created as artificial mountains on which the Pavillon du Rocher is erected in 1779, followed by a grotto, the Ponts de Roches and the Montagne de l'Escargot, 'wild' creations that contrast with the elegance of the Temple de l'Amour of 1778 and the Belvedere, started the same year. A 'rustic' touch is added in the form of the Hameau de la Reine (Queen's hamlet) created by Richard Mique who begins planning it in 1783. This country village of eleven houses built in the Normandy style, has a working farm and dairy in an estate which in 1776 is closed to the public 'by order of the Queen'.

At Versailles, the remodelling of the Bosquet des Bains d'Apollon is completed in 1780 on the design of the landscape painter Hubert Robert. The sculptural groups of Apollo Tended by Nymphs and the Horses of the Sun, originally made for Louis XIV's Grotte de Thétys, are finally moved into a new grotto designed by Hubert Robert and the architect Jean-François Heurtier and built in the bosquet.

## The French Revolution, Versailles appropriated by the nation

1789–1889: On 5 October, 1789, the Parisian mob brings the royal family from Versailles to Paris, but the palace guards and garden staff remain. After the King's execution on 21 January, 1793, there is talk of ploughing the land and using it for farming. However no such extreme measures are taken. Despite the Petit Trianon being sacked, the Queen's former gardener, Antoine Ricard, manages to persuade the Convention to issue a decree stating that it is necessary for the Republic to preserve the royal houses and gardens, 'to create establishments useful to agriculture and the arts'. The gardens are more or less officially opened up to the public, with an inn at the Petit Trianon, a café in the Pavillon Français and dancing in the Jardin Français. Fruit trees are planted beneath the château and around the Grand Canal, the parterres are turned into kitchen gardens and there are plans to sell the trees in the park. The damage is halted when Napoleon I takes an interest in Versailles. He evicts all the occupants, legal tenants or not. If the new emperor ever cherished the idea of establishing his seat of power in this former royal residence, he begins by using the Grand Trianon as his private residence, and little is changed in the gardens, which he restores. He later installs his mother in the newly decorated Grand Trianon, gives the Petit Trianon to his sister, and undertakes the restoration of the Hameau de la Reine for Marie-Antoinette's niece, the Empress Marie-Louise, which is once again opened on

25 August, 1811 for her name day, the feast of St Louis, the patron saint of the kings of the Ancien Régime. The only change made to Versailles during the brief reign of Louis XVIII – the younger brother of Louis XVI who mounted the throne in 1815 – is the new Jardin du Roi, created in 1817 by Alex Dufour, which is laid out as an English-style garden surrounded by allées.

Louis-Philippe, 'King of the French', however, has plans for Versailles. In 1837 the château is turned into a museum dedicated 'to all the glories of France', but his garden projects only consist of blundering interventions and ill-advised modifications.

Under the Second Empire, new cuts are made and replanting starts in 1860, carrying on into 1862 and 1863. Much of the work, however, is undone by the hurricane of 1870, which also wrecks the rows of trees along the Tapis Vert. War, the Prussian occupation and the Paris Commune prevent any further renovation before 1883; but on 5 May, 1889, the Third Republic celebrates the centenary of the reunion of the Etats Généraux (States-General) with grand public festivities at the Bassin de Neptune.

## From the twentieth century to the new millennium

1990–99: A century on from the replanting programme of the Third Republic, the gardens and park have reached maturity and the grounds are admired by millions of visitors from all over the world. A large amount of restoration work is carried out on the interior of the château, but expert analysis of the restoration needed in the grounds is made following the first storm of 1990. Previous projects have nearly always come back to Le Nôtre's designs, often forgetting the changes made by Louis XIV and his successors. Louis XIV's gardens reflect so strongly the mark of their creator that the aim of any restoration becomes obvious: to return to the glory of 1700–1715, in the symmetry of fashioned layouts and the elaborate fantasies of vanished scenery. The work undertaken during the 1990s is based on documents of the period and on archaeological research. In 1991 trees are felled in the two northern bosquets and the Allée d'Eau is replanted and restored to its original state; between 1986 and 1989 the rows of trees in the Allées des Saisons (Allée de l'Eté, Allée du Printemps, Allée de l'Automne and Allée de l'Hiver) are replanted and recover the symmetry of Le Nôtre's pleached hedges; in 1997 the Bosquet de l'Encelade is restored with its trellises and shrubs in ornamental vases, and even its sandstone fountains; the realignment of the Allée Royale or Tapis Vert in 1998 brings back the original scope of the *grande perspective*, thanks to rows of pleached sweet chestnut trees, in the spirit of Le Nôtre, who hated restricted views.

If this work needed justifying, it was certainly done so by the storm that hit Versailles towards the end of 1999, blowing down all the old trees in tragic disarray. Teams and resources are immediately made available to give life back to the open-air museum of the gardens of Versailles. In early 2001 the Parterre de l'Orangerie regains Le Nôtre's original design; in 2002 the Quinconce du Nord and du Midi become once more the Bosquet du Dauphin and Bosquet de la Girandole.

As for the Petit Trianon, which represents life after Versailles, a decision is taken to restore it as it was when Marie-Antoinette was forced to leave it on 5 October, 1789. In 1992 the Jardin Français, designed by Gabriel, is recovered and the changes that were made to the parterres before the French Revolution are kept. The Jardin Anglais, which suffered the most in the 1999 storm, is being restored, but the hamlet – carefully restored in 1950 – still bears witness to the 'rustic' pleasures so sought after in the last years of the Ancien Régime.

And so the story of the gardens of Versailles goes on, living gardens that can only be preserved through nurture, growth, regeneration…

# Further Details
## On places and works mentioned

**The château and gardens**

Seen from the town, the château presents an expanse of stonework. The Cour de Marbre (**I**) is followed by the Galerie Basse, which opens onto the gardens. Beyond that, the *grande perspective* draws the eye towards the horizon, but the great allées, parterres and changes of level created by André Le Nôtre, also afford a variety of views of the château, from west to east, south to north, and north to south. The château, designed by Louis Le Vau and continued by Jules Hardouin-Mansart, lends itself equally well to the intricate play of shadows and light 'created' by Le Nôtre. The rising sun subtly lights up the windows while, at sunset, it highlights the façade and the statues on the great terrace, which converse with the allegorical figures of the Parterre d'Eau (**215, 219**): the Apollo Belvedere and the Dordogne by Antoine Coysevox.

Illustrations I, 4, 25, 49, 137, 138, 139, 142, 146, 147, 215, 216–219

**The Bassin d'Apollon**
**(Apollo Fountain)**

Situated at the west end of the Tapis Vert, before the start of the Grand Canal, the Bassin d'Apollon takes its name from a lead sculpture by Jean-Baptiste Tuby, started in 1668, representing Apollo on his chariot (**5–8, 132, 206**), which is drawn by four horses, and surrounded by four tritons and dolphins. The statue was gilded at Versailles and placed in position in 1671. Around the bassin, on the side of the Grand Canal, statues of Ino and Melicertes by Pierre Granier are arranged in an arc (**80, 81, 82, 144**). Statues also border the Allée d'Apollon which stretches from north to south at the start of the Grand Canal: Pomona by Etienne Le Hongre, Bacchus begun by Jean Dugoulon and completed by Jean-Melchior Raon (**152, 153, 163**), and Spring started by Marc Arcis and completed by Simon Mazière. On either side of the Bassin d'Apollon, perpendicular to the Grand Canal, lie the northern and southern Allées d'Apollon, likewise adorned with statues, including Light by Baldi (**154**).

Illustrations 2, 3, 5, 6, 7, 8, 27, 28, 29, 30, 32, 33, 78, 80, 81, 82, 132, 144, 152, 153, 154, 163, 179, 201, 202, 204, 206, 207

## The Grand Canal

Excavation work began in 1668 and was completed in 1679. This 1,650 metre-long stretch of water ends at the Etoile Royale (**76, 118, 211**), with two arms forming a transverse axis leading from the old Ménagerie (no longer extant) to the Grand Trianon and the Bassin du Fer à Cheval, framed by a magnificent staircase (**10, 22, 43, 47, 88–90**). Used for illuminations and musical pleasure-trips during the Ancien Régime, it held an entire flotilla of model warships, rowing boats, gondolas and the King's galley. It is bordered by rows of tall trees, formerly elms, now linden trees. The Grand Canal offers changing views of the château according to one's position, the time of day and the season.

Illustrations 9, 12, 19, 20, 22, 24, 43, 47, 76, 88–90, 116, 125, 203, 211, 214

## The *grande perspective* (great perspective)

Designed by André Le Nôtre, the *grande perspective* follows an east-west axis, from the château to the end of the Grand Canal. The nine-kilometre stretch, leading from the château to the end of the canal, was created between 1663 and 1679. It took an enormous programme of excavation and earthwork and the most advanced techniques of the time, along with tens of thousands of men to build and enlarge the Allée Royale (also known as the Tapis Vert), which leads from the Parterre de Latone to the Bassin d'Apollon and the Grand Canal.

Illustrations 13, 14, 17, 70, 114, 115, 209

## The Parterre d'Eau (Water Terrace)

From the Galerie des Glaces and directly below the terrace, one has an immediate view of the mirror pools of the Parterre d'Eau, with the Bassin du Midi and the Bassin du Nord; these are among Le Nôtre's most exceptional creations, not only because of their size, but also because of the play of reflections and changing hues that they

389

produce. The white marble rims are decorated with sixteen bronze statues representing the rivers and tributaries of France, along with eight nymphs. The Dordogne by Antoine Coysevox (**72**) and the Marne (**148, 165, 216, 219**) by Etienne Le Hongre, are on the north edge. The Loiret (**143**) by Thomas Regnaudin lies on the south edge. On the corners of the bassin are groups of children, including the group with a child holding a bird (**164**) and the dolphin group (**166**) by Simon Mazière.

Illustrations 56, 72, 142, 143, 145, 148, 164, 166, 216, 219

### The north-south axis

The axis of the *grande perspective* ends in front of the château in a vast north-south axis. A huge turf parterre with topiary borders is named the Parterre du Nord because of its northern position. At its centre lie the two Bassins des Couronnes (**34,158**), adorned by lead statues Jean-Baptiste Tuby and Etienne Le Hongre. Other statues in the parterre include the Crouching Venus, after Antoine Coysevox (**57**), the Choleric by

Jacques Houzeau (**155**), which were included by Louis XIV in what was known as the *grande commande* (great commission), issued in 1674 to the best artists of the period. It followed a rigorous iconographic programme: the four seasons, the four continents, the four humours of man, as well as other allegories.

To the south, the Parterre du Midi overlooks the Orangerie, which only comes into view from the balustrade of the château's terrace, and is reached by the Cent Marches staircase (**96, 182**); the view stretches towards the Pièce d'Eau des Suisses, named after the regiment that excavated it.

Illustrations 15, 16, 18, 34, 51, 57, 96, 102, 104, 108, 155, 158, 182

### The Cabinets des Animaux (Animal Arbours)

On either side of the west end of the Parterre d'Eau stand two bassins, the Cabinets des Animaux, which remind us that Versailles was once a hunting ground. In the northern Cabinet are two bronze groups, one by Cornelius van Cleve, and the other by Jean Raon (1687), depicting a lion bringing down a wild boar (**64, 135, 136**). Nearby is the statue of Daybreak (**145**) by Gaspard Marsy. Opposite the northern Cabinet, the southern Cabinet displays bronzes by Jacques Houzeau (1687), depicting a tiger overcoming a bear and a hound attacking a stag (**65**).

Illustrations 64, 65, 135, 136

### The southern Bassins des Saisons (Fountains of the Seasons)

In the Allée de l'Hiver (Winter), south of the Tapis Vert (Allée Royale), stands the Bassin de Saturne with a statue of Winter in gilded lead by François Girardon, made between 1675 and 1677 (**173, 174, 180, 181**) from a design by Charles Le Brun. The Bassin de Bacchus in the Allée de l'Automne (Autumn), is decorated with a statue of Bacchus by Gaspard and Balthazar Marsy. (**173, 174**).

Illustrations 173, 174, 180, 181

### The northern Bassins des Saisons (Fountains of the Seasons)

In the Allée de l'Eté (Summer), to the north of the Tapis Vert (Allée Royale),

stands the Bassin de Cérès with the sculptural group of gilded lead (1672–75) by Thomas Regnaudin (**31, 176, 178**), from a design by Charles Le Brun. The Bassin de Flore in the Allée du Printemps (Spring) is ornamented by a group sculpted by Jean-Baptiste Tuby. (**171, 175**).

Illustrations 26, 31, 156, 171, 175, 176, 178

### The Bassin and Parterre de Latone (Latona Fountain and Terrace)

The Bassin de Latone is situated below the Parterre d'Eau and is flanked by two other bassins known as the Fontaines des Lézards (**73**), designed by the Marsy brothers, Balthazar and Gaspard, and executed between 1678 and 1680; the marble figure represents Latona holding her children Apollo and Diana, gods of the sun and moon, children of Jupiter. Mocked by Lycian peasants, Latona turns to the king of Olympia who transforms the wicked people into frogs, lizards and tortoises, here sculpted in gilded lead.

From May to October, the flower beds, bordered by clipped yew, are embellished with orange trees in planters taken out of the Orangerie (**66–69, 71**) after the winter. The Parterre de Latone (**79, 103, 109, 140, 141, 157, 162**), which is accessed by a majestic staircase is framed by two gentle slopes forming a crescent shape adorned with statues, including the nymph with a shell. Illustrations 21, 35, 36, 50, 66–69, 71, 73, 79, 103, 109, 133, 140, 141, 157, 162

### The Bassin de Neptune (Neptune Fountain)

It took over a century to build the Bassin de Neptune at the northern end of the gardens. André Le Nôtre designed its semi-circular shape in 1678 and oversaw the beginning of its construction, which was taken over by Jules Hardouin-Mansart, from 1679 to 1684. In the same year, the retaining wall was decorated with basins and shells and ornamented with twenty-two gilded lead vases (**52, 183**). The hydraulic system comprises twenty-two lances on the rim of the retaining wall, another twenty-two in the vases and six jets of water in the bassin. However, work on the project

was halted and, between 1733 and 1738, it fell to Ange-Jacques Gabriel to almost entirely rebuild it. The central group of Neptune and Amphitrite (**126**) was executed in 1740 by Lambert Sigisbert Adam; Oceanus (**127**) is the work of Jean-Baptiste Lemoyne, and the group of two cupids riding two giant dragons is by Edme Bouchardon. This fountain comprises ninety-nine water features in total. Near the bassin stands the allegorical group of Fame writing the history of the King by Domenico Guidi (**161**).
Illustrations 38, 41, 52, 126, 127, 161, 183

### The Bosquet des Rocailles (Rocaille Grove)

The Bosquet des Rocailles was formerly known as the Salle de Bal (ballroom), as people would dance in the central arena; it was created by André Le Nôtre in 1680. A cascade runs over steps embellished with burr-stone and shells from the Red Sea and the Indian Ocean.
Illustrations 42

## The Bassin du Miroir (Mirror Fountain)

The Bassin du Miroir, seen here before the storm in 1999, is all that remains of the Ile Royale; the Apollo Pothos is an antique statue.
Illustrations 48, 55

## The Petit Trianon (Small Trianon) and the Hameau de la Reine (Queen's Hamlet)

The new, or Petit Trianon was originally a botanical garden created by Louis XV at the instigation of Madame de Pompadour. Bernard de Jussieu constructed greenhouses, which were considered the most modern in Europe. But after the death of Louis XV, the flower beds and greenhouses were replaced with an Anglo-Chinese garden (197), according to Marie-Antoinette's taste. The Belvedere (53) was erected on a mound overlooking a small lake. The Temple de l'Amour (159) was built in 1778 by the Queen's favourite architect, Richard Mique; at the centre of this circular edifice is a replica of Edme Bouchardon's group depicting Cupid carving a bow out of Hercules'

club (160), the original of which is in the Louvre. The Hameau de la Reine (74) was designed for Marie-Antoinette by Richard Mique.

## The Grand Trianon (Great Trianon)

This is also called the Trianon de Marbre because of the marble pilasters surrounding the peristyle (185, 186). Under Louis XIV the building was dedicated to flowers and, according to Madame de Maintenon, they were so numerous and their scent so powerful as to cause discomfort. Flower beds still exist, but the flowers are in pots, allowing them to be easily varied. The transverse arm of the Grand Canal is visible from the garden balustrade. Inside the balustrade lies the Bassin du Plat-Fond (198), ornamented with dragons sculpted by Jean Hardy, the same artist who created the nymphs in the Bassin de l'Amphithéâtre or Salle des Antiques (199, 200). The Trianon-sous-bois wing of the pavilion (75) was reserved for the King's family; during Charles de Gaulle's government it was used by the head of state. The gardens of the Grand Trianon back onto open fields.

### The Salle des Marronniers (Chestnut Tree Clearing)

Designed by Jules Hardouin-Mansart in 1704, the Salle des Marronniers replaced Le Nôtre's Galerie des Antiques, while preserving its long and thin shape, as well as its antique busts and statues, including one of Marcus Aurelius (151); marble fountains stand at each opening (58, 59).

### The Bosquet de l'Encelade (Enceladus Grove)

Created in 1675 by Le Nôtre, the Bosquet de l'Encelade was restored to its original state in 1998. The central fountain has a gilded lead statue by Gaspard Marsy, representing the punishment of Enceladus by Jupiter for attempting to climb Mount Olympus.

### The Bosquet de l'Obélisque (Obelisk Grove)

Formerly the Salles des Festins designed by Le Nôtre, the Bosquet de l'Obélisque owes its present form to Jules Hardouin-Mansart, who transformed it from 1704 to 1705. The central bassin is decorated by a crown of reeds from which rise 231 jets of water.

### The Bosquet des Dômes (Grove of the Domed Pavilions)

After its creation by Le Nôtre in 1675, two small pavilions were built in the bosquet between 1677 and 1678 and given domical roofs, hence the name of the bosquet; the pavilions contained the sculptures which are now in the Bosquet des Bains d'Apollon, but were destroyed in 1820. The balustrade is decorated with forty-four reliefs executed by François Girardon, Pierre Mazeline and Gilles Guérin.

### The Bosquet de la Colonnade (Colonnade Grove)

This was the first bosquet built by Jules Hardouin-Mansart in 1685; its marble architecture is a radical departure from Le Nôtre's preference for plants and trelliswork. Thirty-two differently coloured marble columns, coupled with thirty-two square columns in Languedoc marble, form a perfect circle measuring thirty-two metres in diameter, and support the arches and the white marble arcade surmounted by thirty-two urns. Under each arch stand wide fountains of white marble. Girardon's masterpiece, The Rape of Prosperine, was installed in the centre of the bosquet in 1700 (**84**). The present group is a cast of the original (executed between 1677 and 1679), which is kept in storage.

Illustrations 83, 84, 187, 189

### The Bosquet des Bains d'Apollon (Grove of the Baths of Apollo)

A sculptural group of Apollo tended by nymphs (**85, 86**), was executed by Girardon and Regnaudin between 1666 and 1672. The Horses of the Sun comprises two groups: the rearing horse is by the Marsy brothers (**87**), and the watered horse is by Gilles Guérin. Commissioned to decorate the Grotte de Thétys, which was destroyed in 1684, these were only placed in the Bosquet des Bains d'Apollon, designed by Hubert Robert, after 1775 when the garden was replanted by Louis XVI.

Illustrations 85, 87

### The Bosquet de la Reine (Queen's Grove)

Seen from the staircase of the Orangerie, before the storm in 1999, the bosquet replaced a labyrinth by Le Nôtre.

Illustrations 95, 208

### The Cent Marches and the Orangerie (Hundred Steps and Orangery)

The Cent Marches staircase is, in fact, made up of over 200 steps, as the eastern half of the staircase has 103 steps, while the western half has 104. The Orangerie's turf terraces have just been restored to Le Nôtre's original design. From May to October, some of the 1,600 exotic trees, preserved in winter inside the building designed by Jules Hardouin-Mansart, are placed around the central bassin; the Orangerie contains not only orange trees but also pomegranates and bay trees. Certain specimens are over two hundred years old.

Illustrations 51, 96, 98–102, 182

### The Jardin du Roi (King's Garden)

The bosquet of the Jardin du Roi was created by Louis XVIII, who laid it out in the style of a picturesque English garden.

Illustrations 110, 111, 172

### The Bassin du Dragon
### (Dragon Fountain)

Situated at the bottom of the Allée d'Eau, the Bassin du Dragon was decorated with lead statues by the Marsy brothers, illustrating the legend of Python, the terrible snake-dragon conquered by Apollo. Restored in 1889, this decorative scheme, which includes children riding swans, contains few of the original fragments.

Illustrations 37, 128, 131, 134

### The Allée d'Eau (Water Path)

This gently slopes downwards from the cascade known as the Bains des Nymphes de Diane, by Girardon, (149, 150) to the Bassin du Dragon, on the south-north axis of the château. It is commonly known as the Allée des Marmousets (familiar term for little boys) because of the twelve fountains decorated with children, originally executed in gilded lead and painted naturalistically, including the group of three girls and a bird by Pierre Legros the elder and Benoît Massou.

Illustrations 37, 149, 150, 167, 168

### The Bosquet de la Girandole
### (Firework Grove)

This was one of the first bosquets created by Le Nôtre. It already appeared in a garden plan dated 1663. Replanted in the Quinconce du Midi between 1775 and 1776, it was restored to its original state in 2001, along with a term of Minerva inspired by Nicholas Poussin.

Illustrations 192, 194

### The Bosquet du Dauphin
### (Dauphin's Grove)

Parallel to the Bosquet de la Girandole, the Bosquet du Dauphin has also been restored to its original state. The statue of Liberality, after Nicolas Poussin, is one of eleven of the sixteen terms that were ordered by Louis XIV's Finance minister, Nicolas Fouquet, in 1655 for the château of Vaux-le-Vicomte; the King purchased these for Versailles in 1683.

# Glossary of garden terms

**allée**: a path, walk or ride in a garden or park, sometimes bordered by trees or hedges.

**arbour**: a shelter or shady retreat open on one side.

**bassin**: a formal pond or the bowl of a fountain.

**belvedere**: a raised platform or summer house sited to command a fine view.

**berceau**: an arbour covered by trees trained to form a vault or by plants growing over trelliswork.

**bosquet**: a grove or wooded area in a garden, usually with clearings decorated with fountains, statues, etc.

**buffet d'eau**: a stepped fountain with water flowing from vessels placed on the top or on the steps.

**cabinet**: a small enclosure or arbour.

**parterre**: a symmetrical arrangement of formal beds.

**pleaching**: a form of pruning by which the branches of trees are interlaced or intertwined to form a fence.

**potager**: a kitchen garden

**rocaille**: rock and shell decoration.

**salle**: a clearing in a bosquet, larger than a cabinet.

**salle de verdure**: a clearing decorated with plants.

# Index of places and sculptural groups

*Numbers refer to illustrations*

# Acknowledgments

My thanks to those behind the scenes who allowed me to record the effects
of the changing light, moments of supreme honour which I will never forget.
Through photography, I am able to share these moments of intense emotion
with them. I would like to thank:

Pierre Arrizoli-Clémentel, Hubert Asier, Alain Baraton, Michel Baridon,
Bruno Baudry, Christian Bongoat, Patrick Bouchet, Françoise and Michel Buntz,
Jean-François Camp, Jean Cancelier, Jean-Paul Capitani, Christian Caujolle,
Mic Chamblas-Ploton, Joël Cottin, Rachel Coudray, Marc Dumotier, Frédéric Dia,
Pascale Gélys, Géraldine Ghislain, Roger Jouan, Thierry Lamouroux,
Jean-Louis Lebigre, Estelle Lemaître, Ariane de Lestrange, Gabriel Levolo,
John Loring, Isabelle Mariana, Patrick Martin, Gwenola Menou, Sylvie Messinger,
Françoise Nyssen, Gonzague Perney, Bruno Pommier, Bénédicte Poupard,
Gilles Quinqueneau, Michel Racine, Florence Renouf, Yann Rogier,
Sandro Rumney, Béatrix Saule, Lucienne Strbella.

Laurent Roussel, President of Actibail
Member of the Ing Group.